FRIED LINES

VOL 0 All Over the Place

▶ Geared Up

▶ Go Cheese Go

▶ Pocket Power

▶ Sea Spiral

▶ Climb Into the
  Window Zone

ILLUSTRATED BY: Ben Friedrich
FRIEDLINES.COM

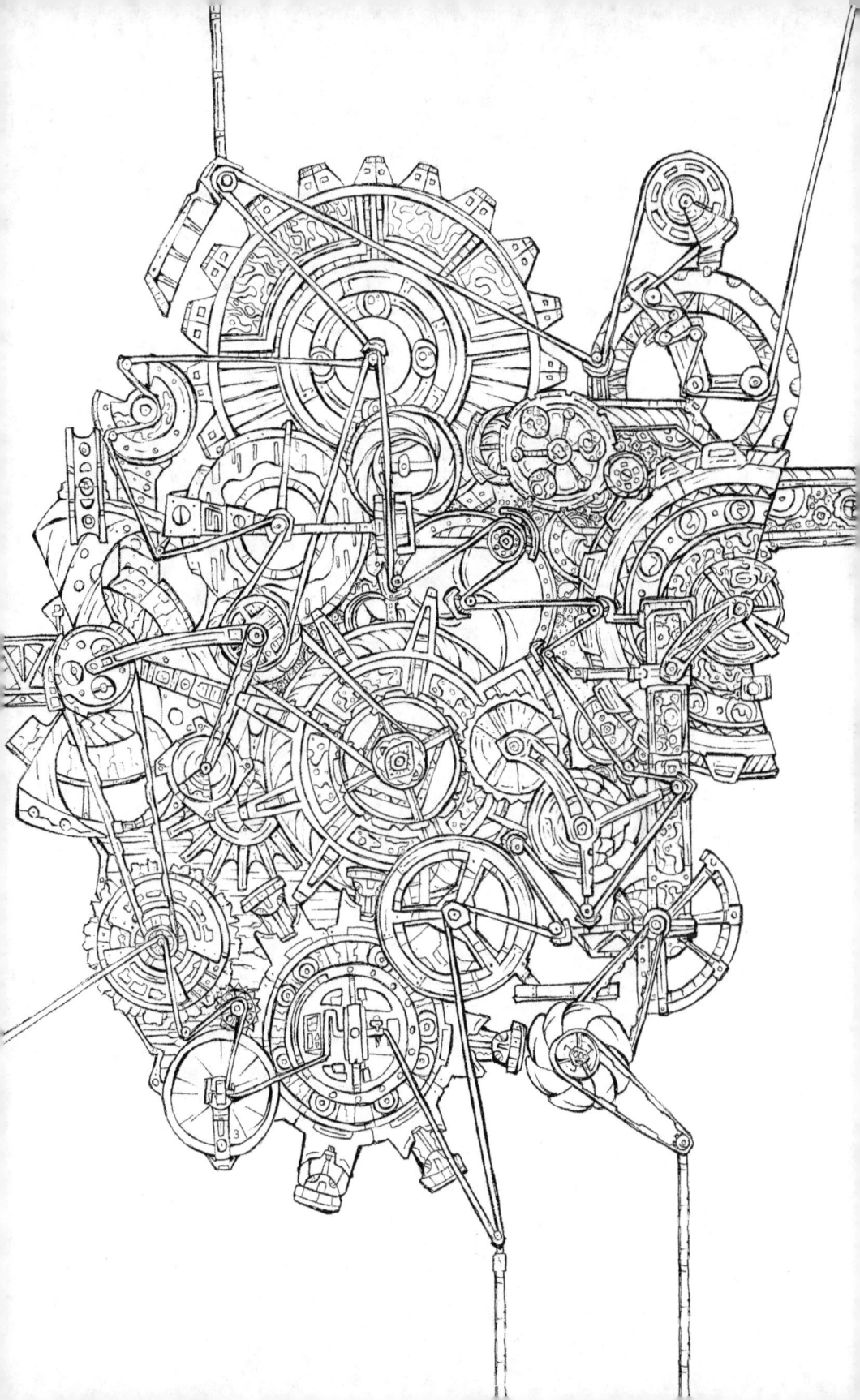

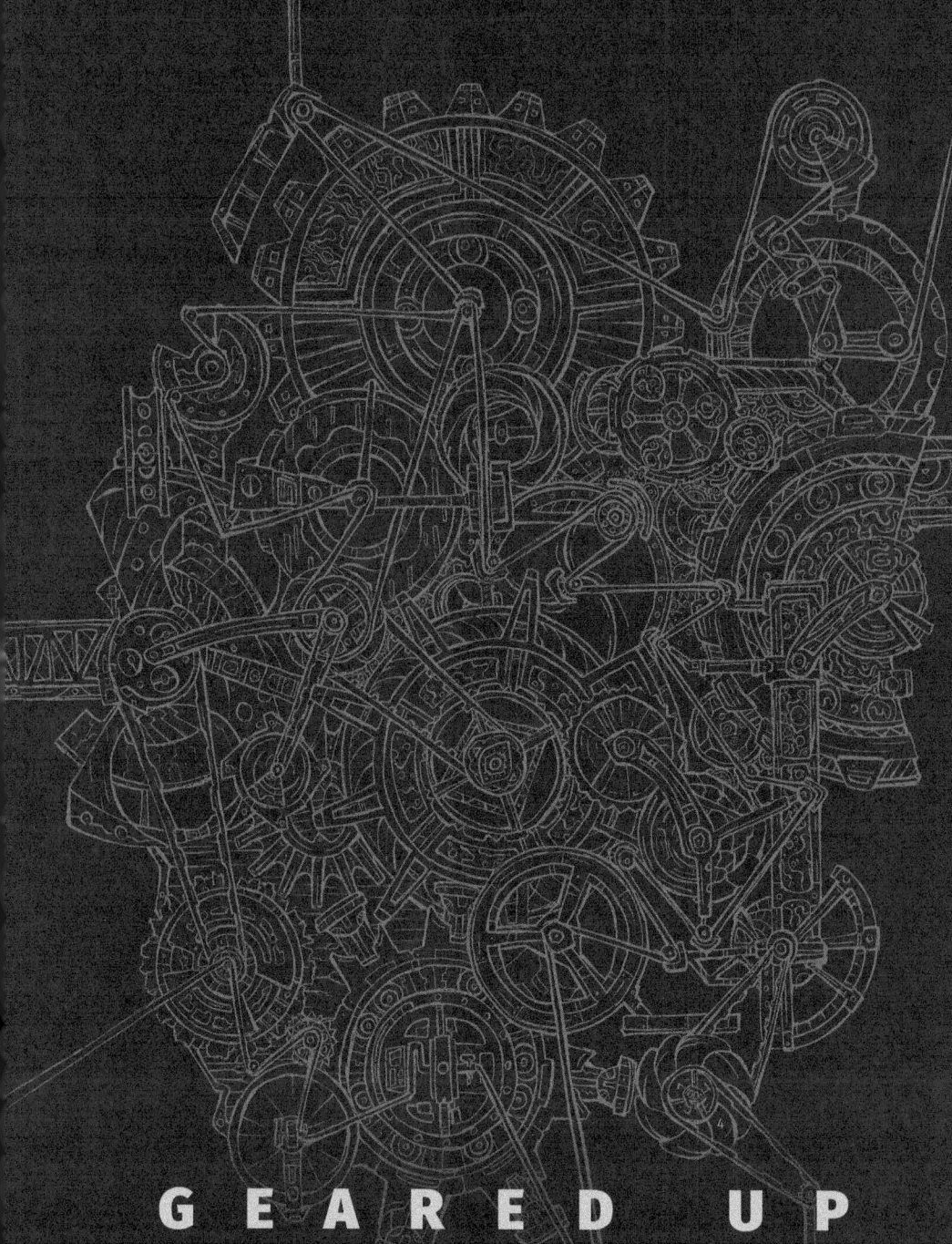

GEARED UP

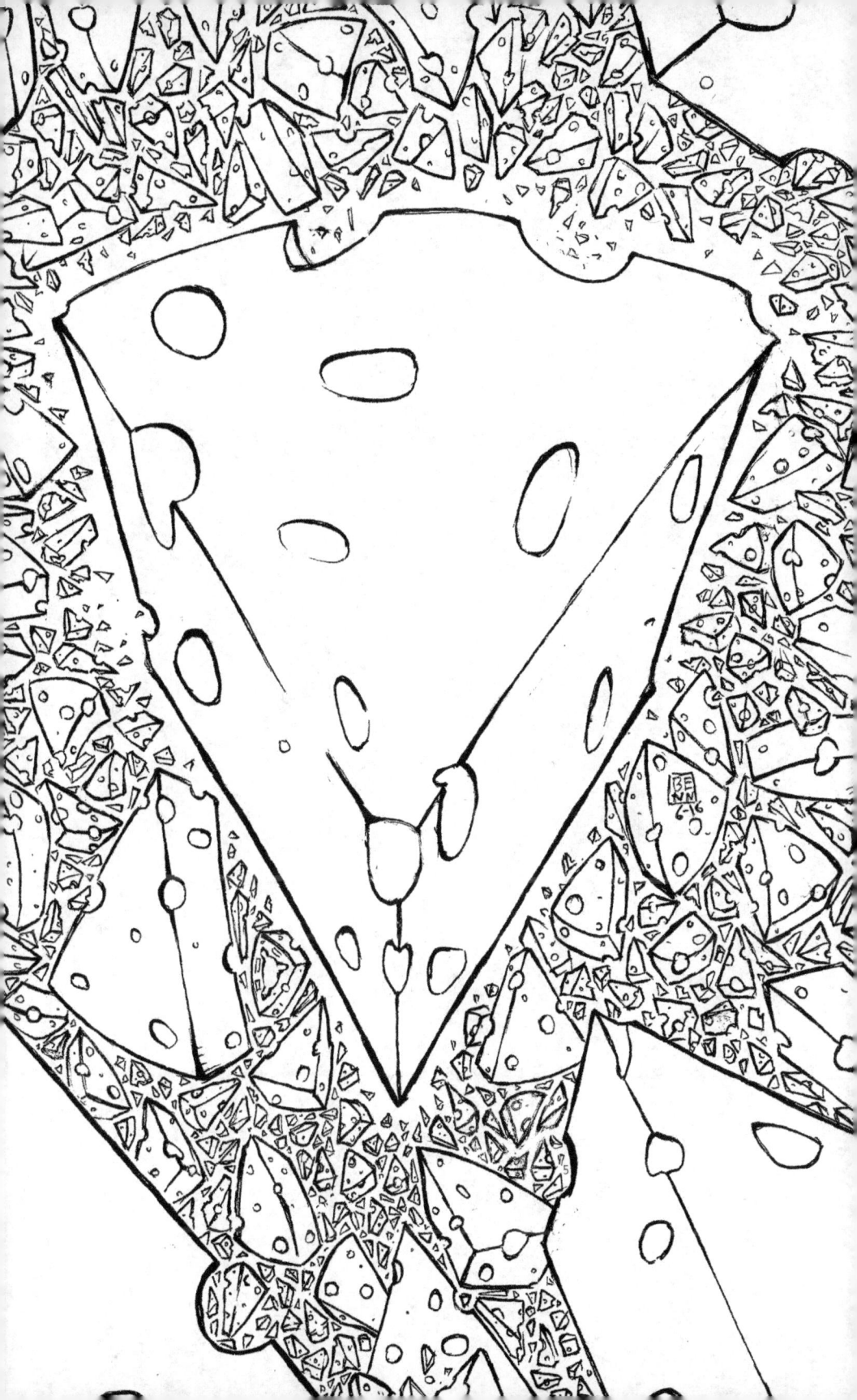

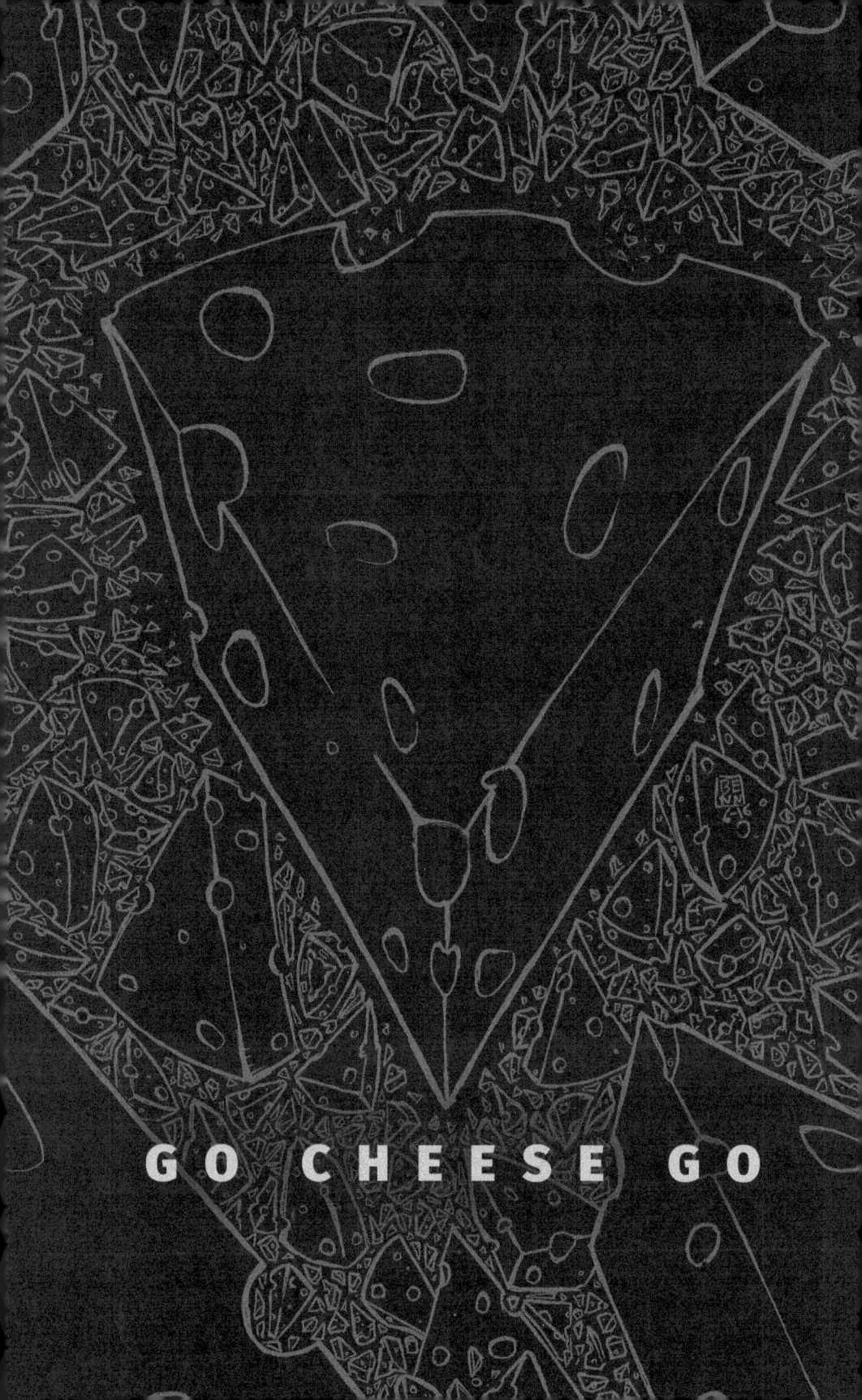

GO CHEESE GO

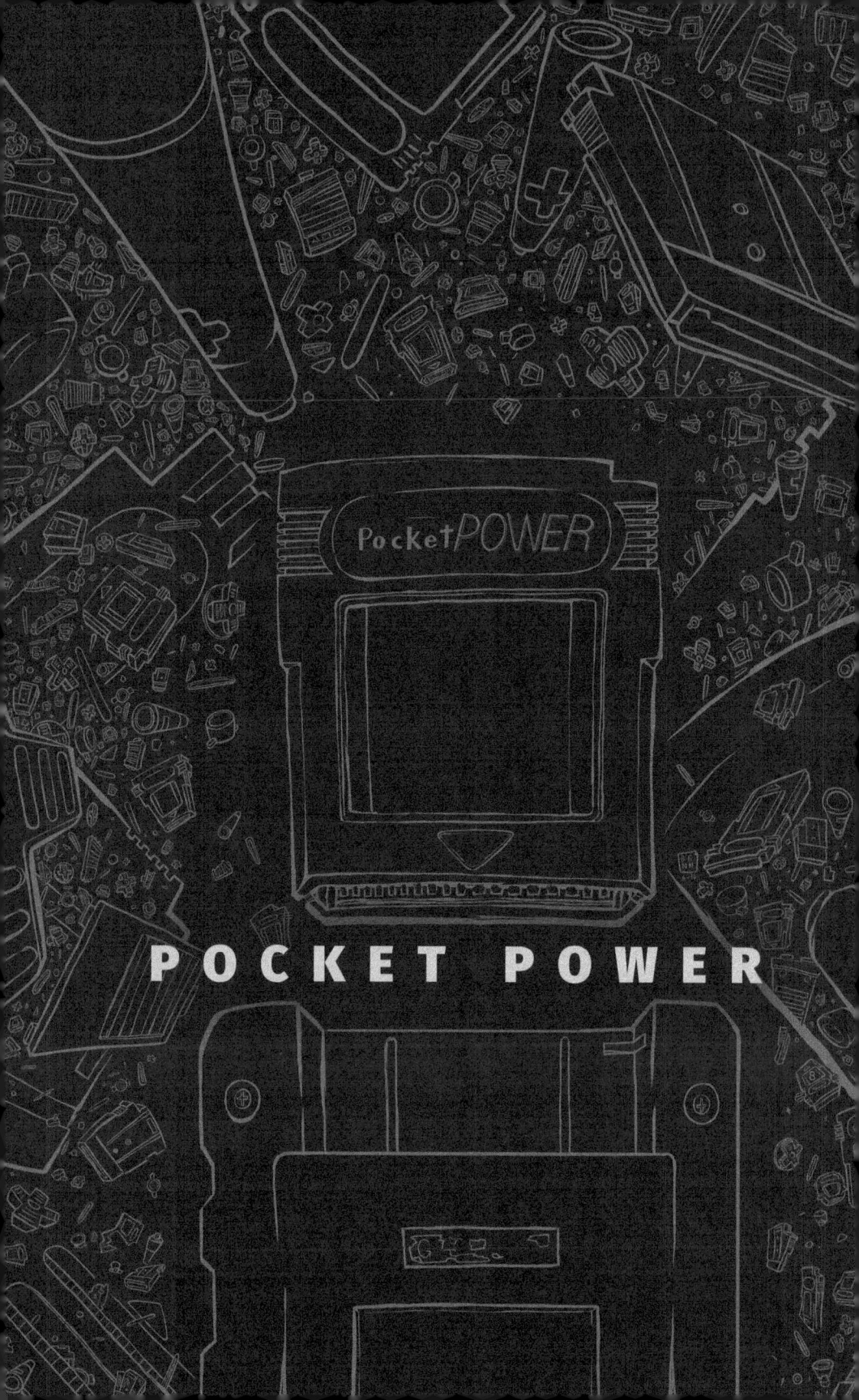

POCKET POWER

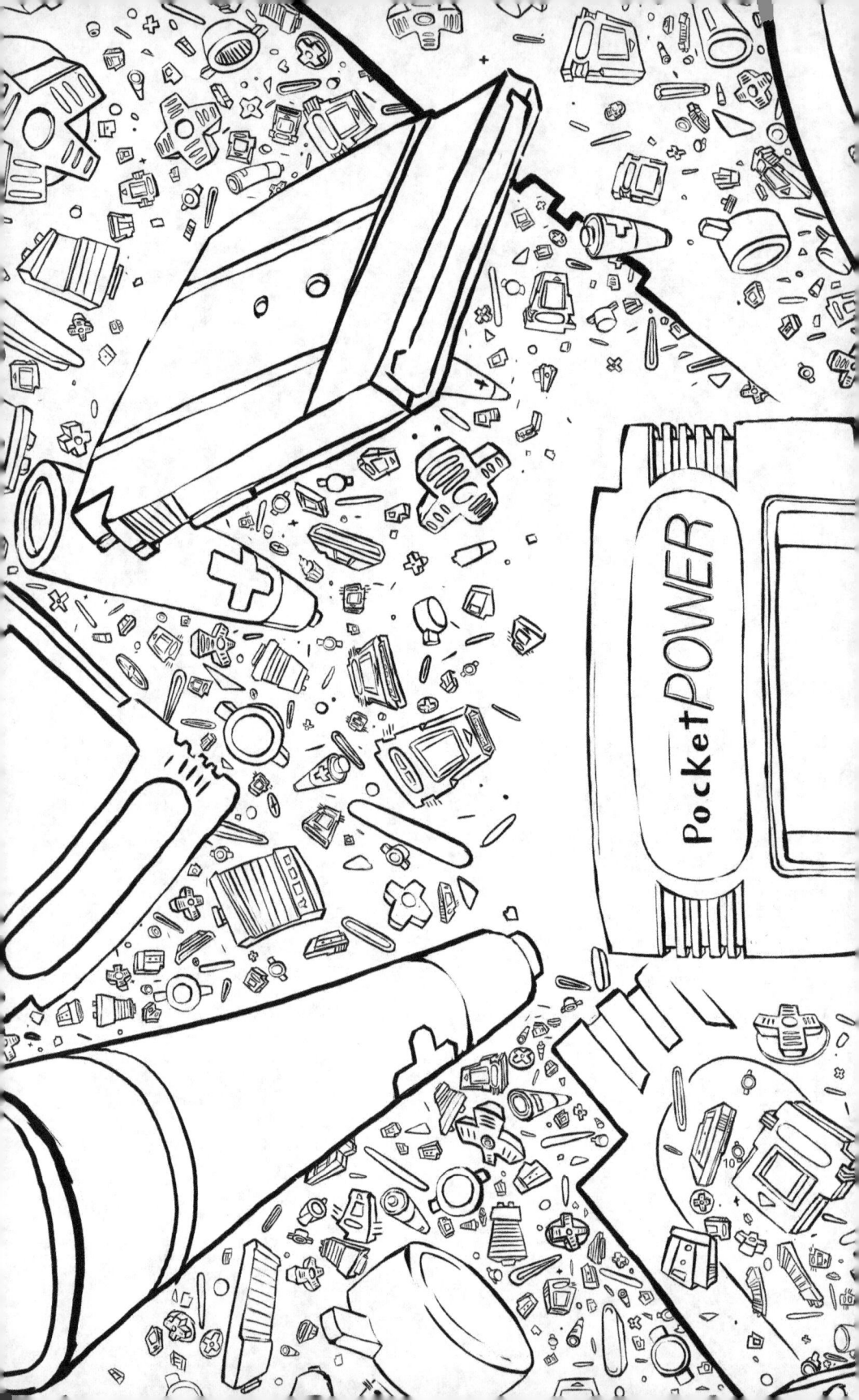

PocketPOWER

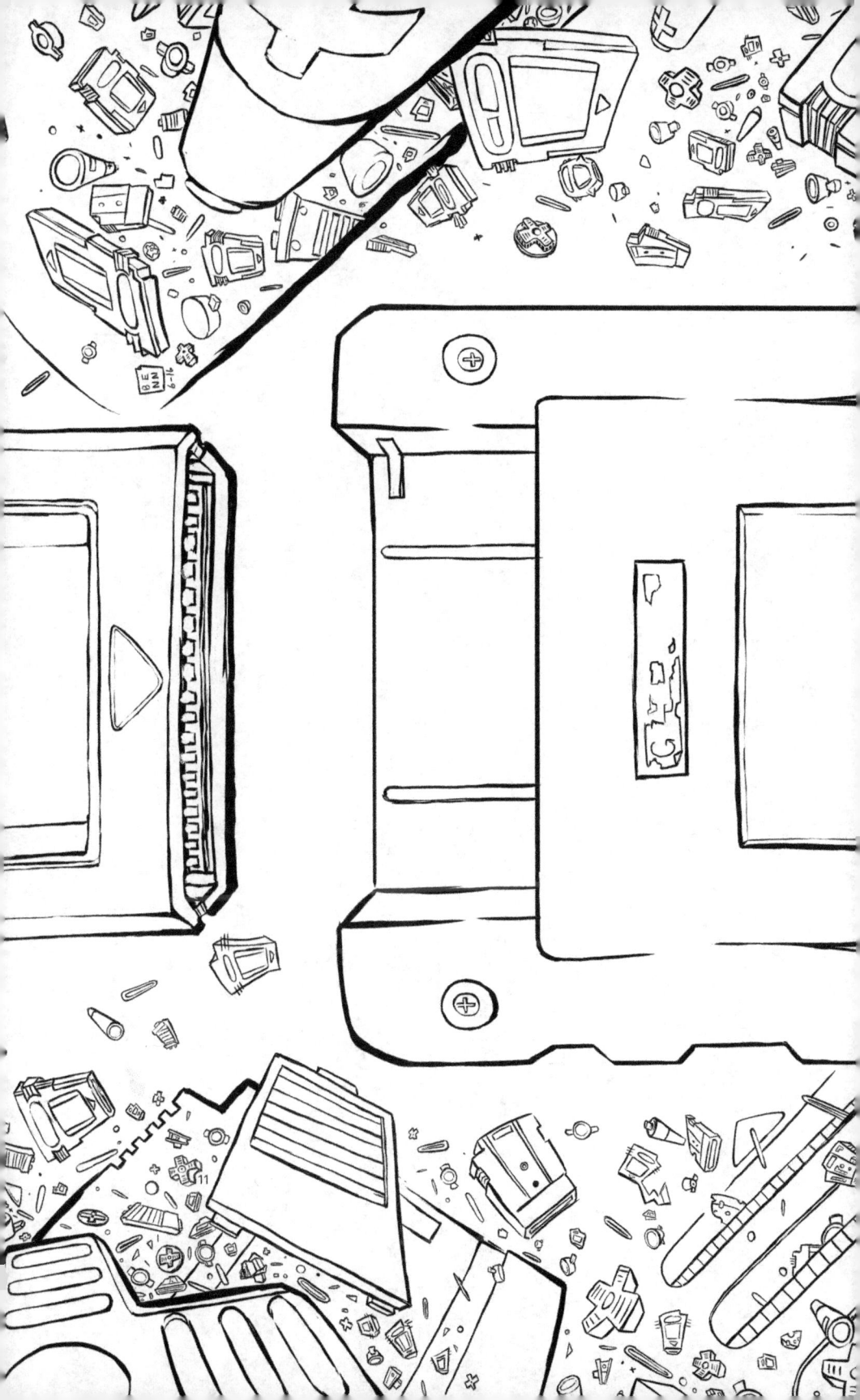

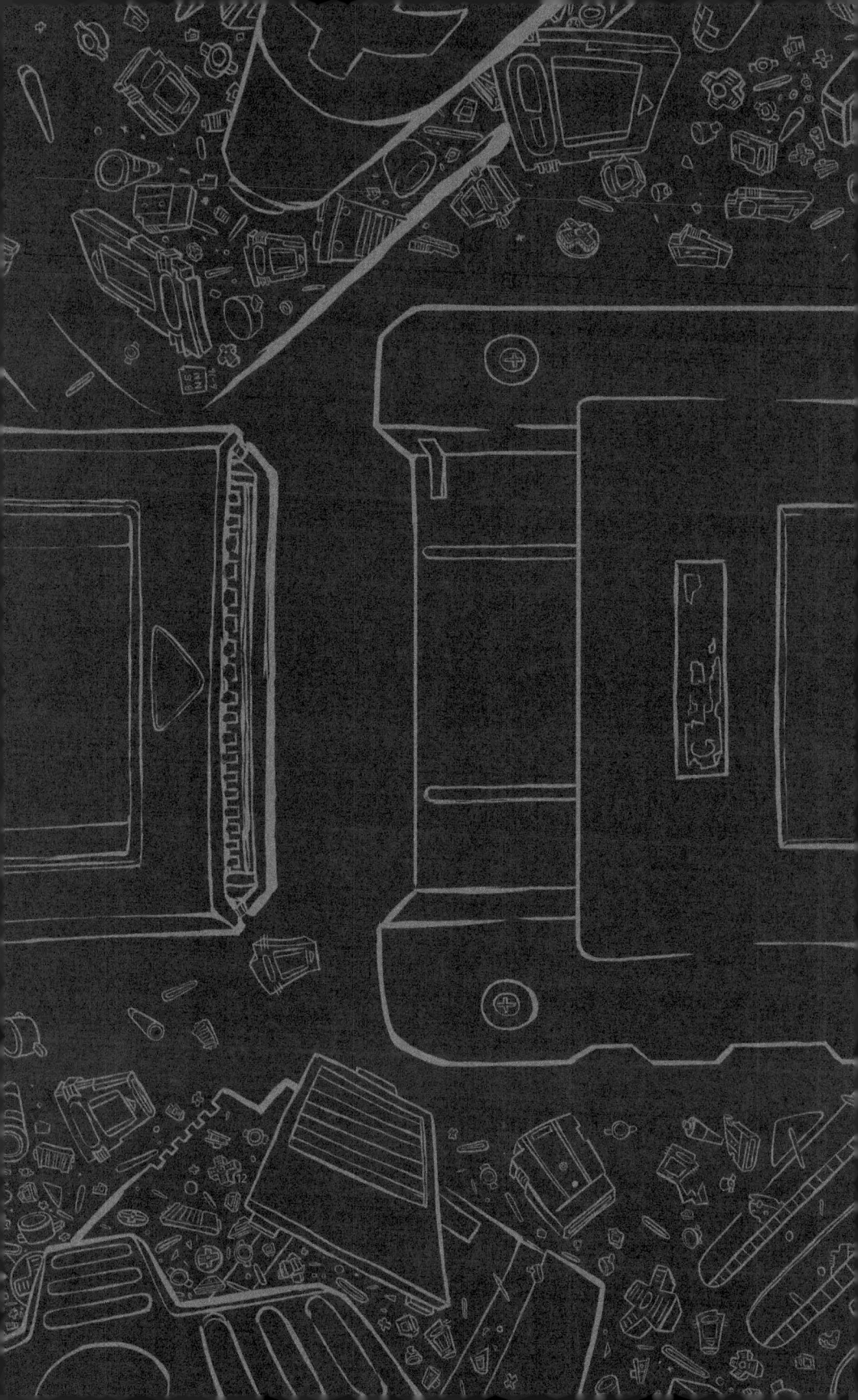

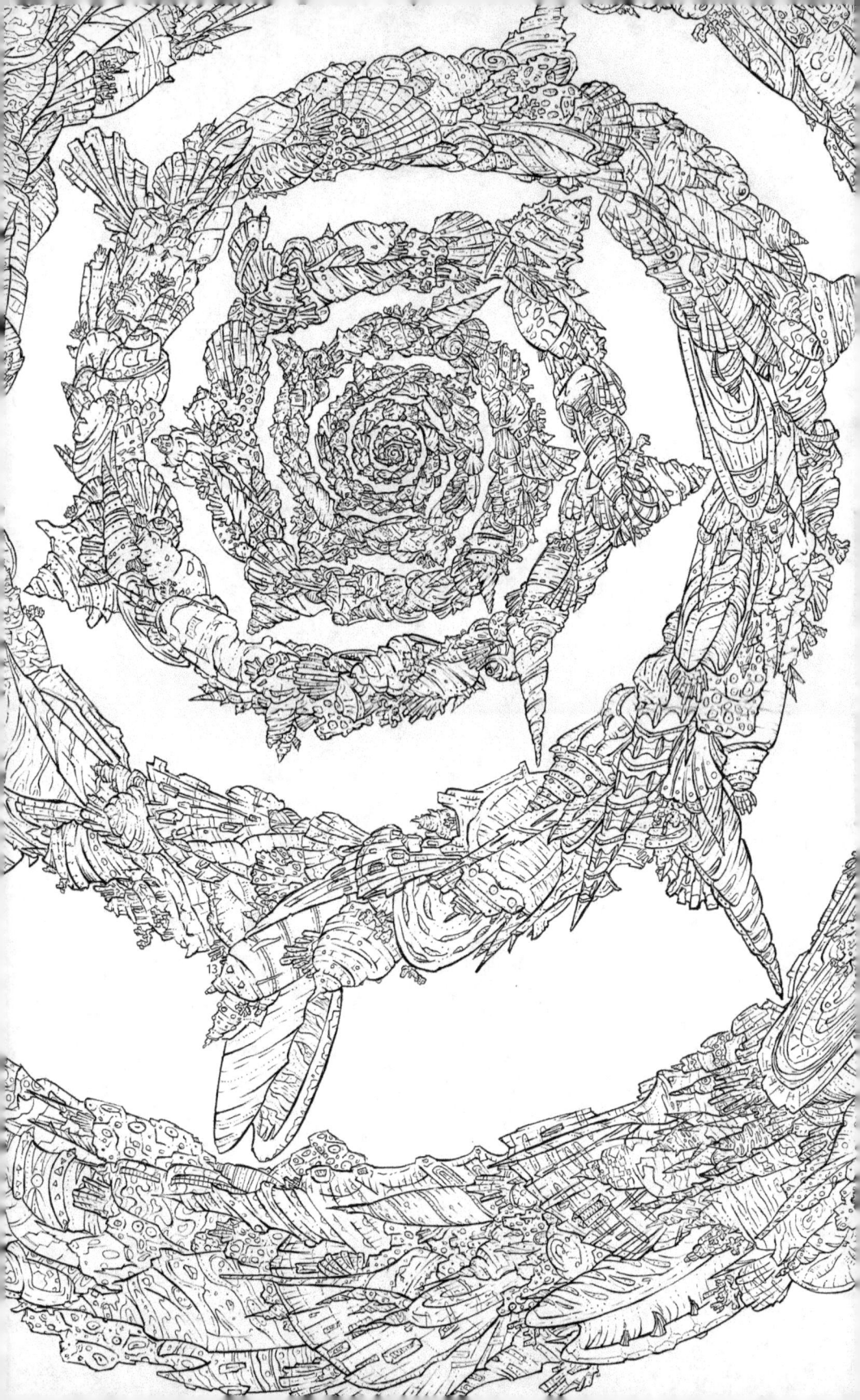

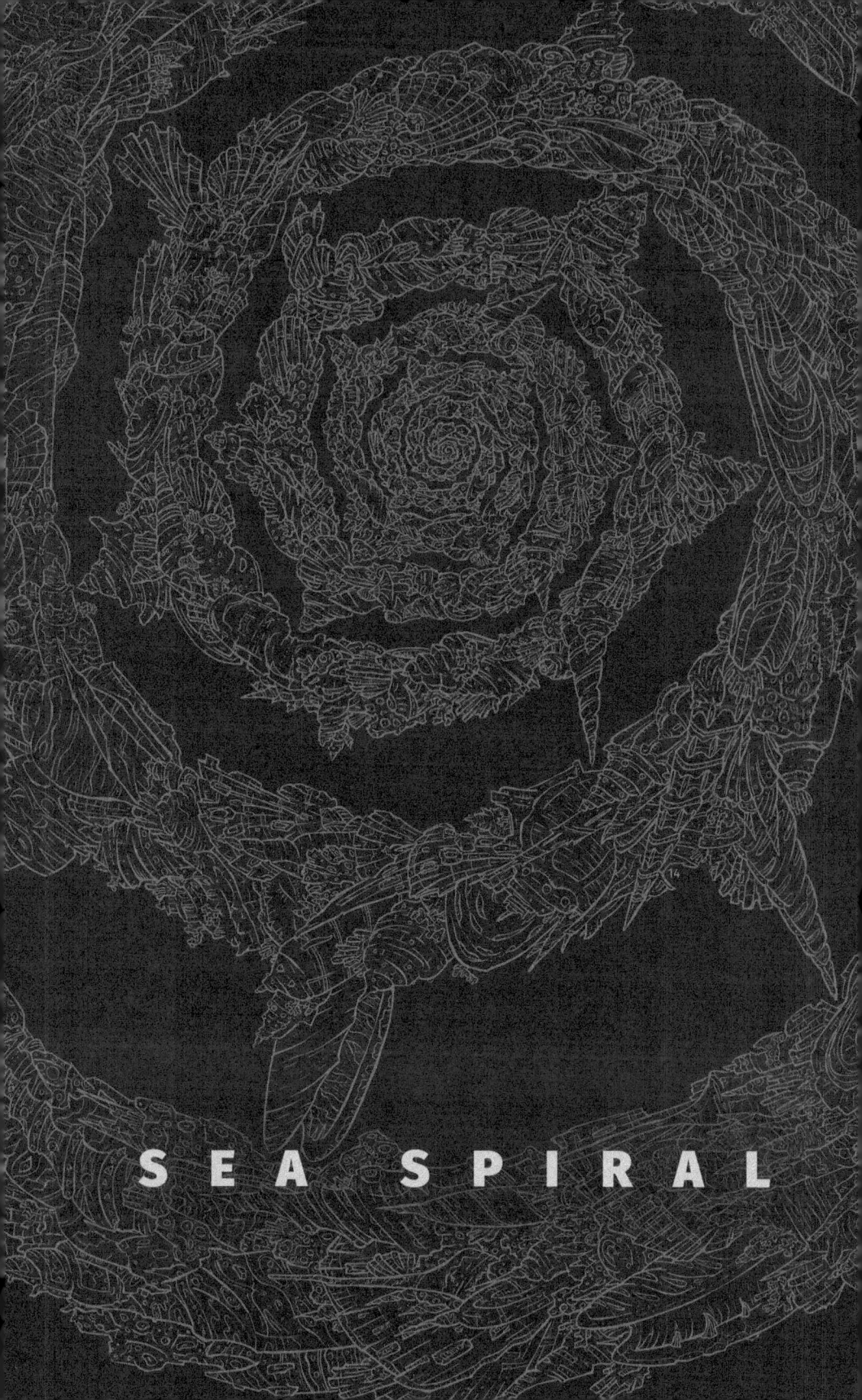

SEA SPIRAL

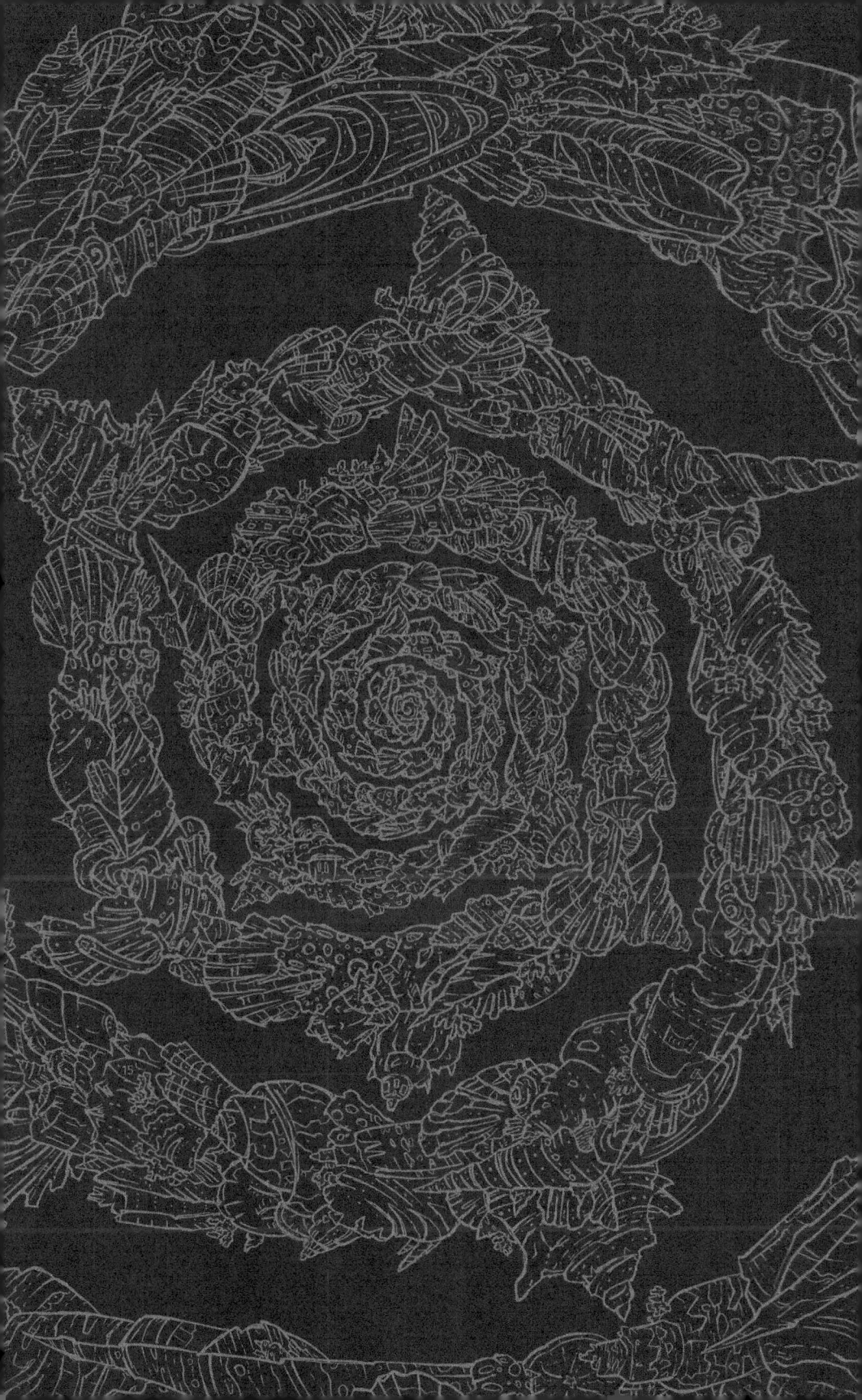

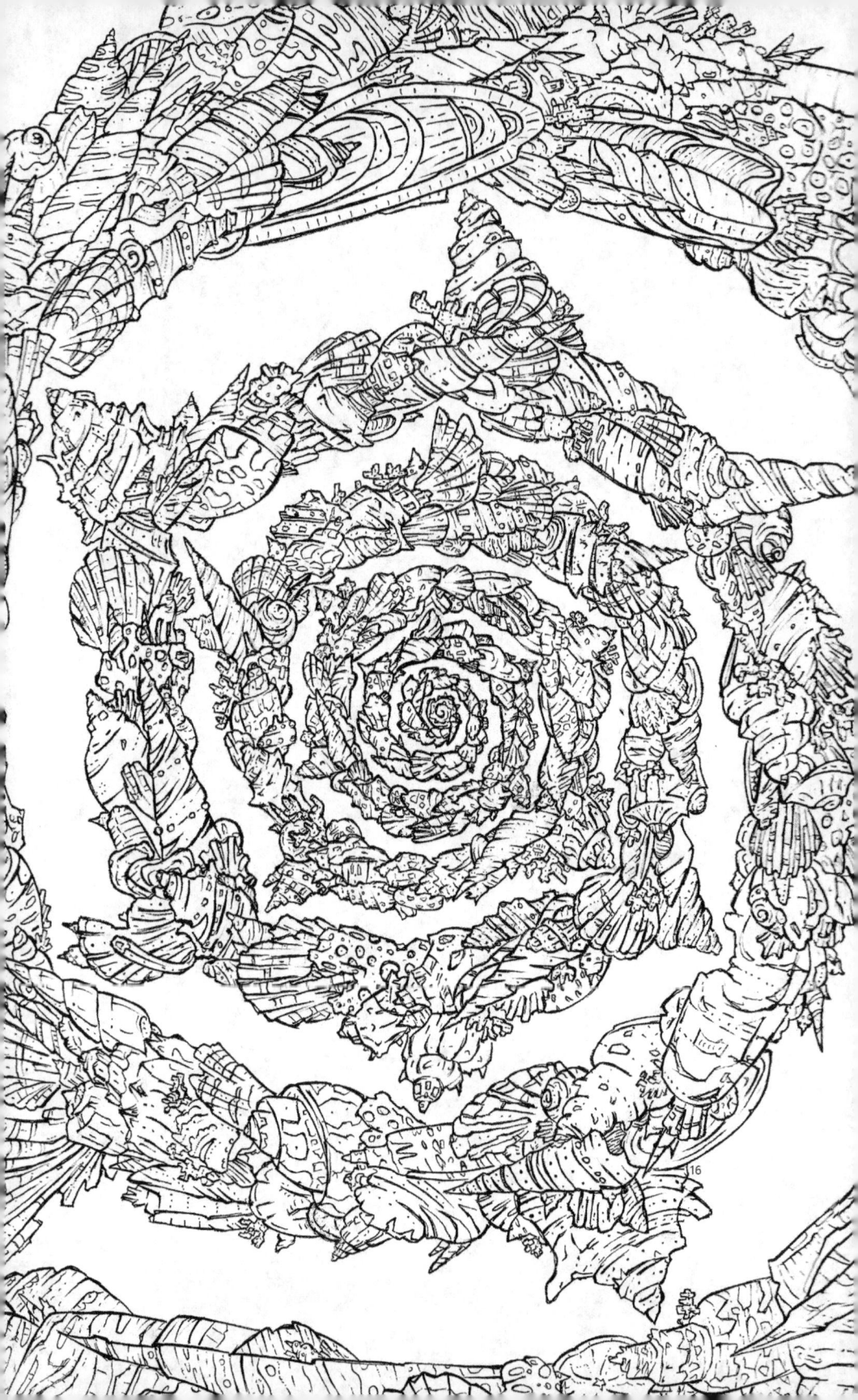

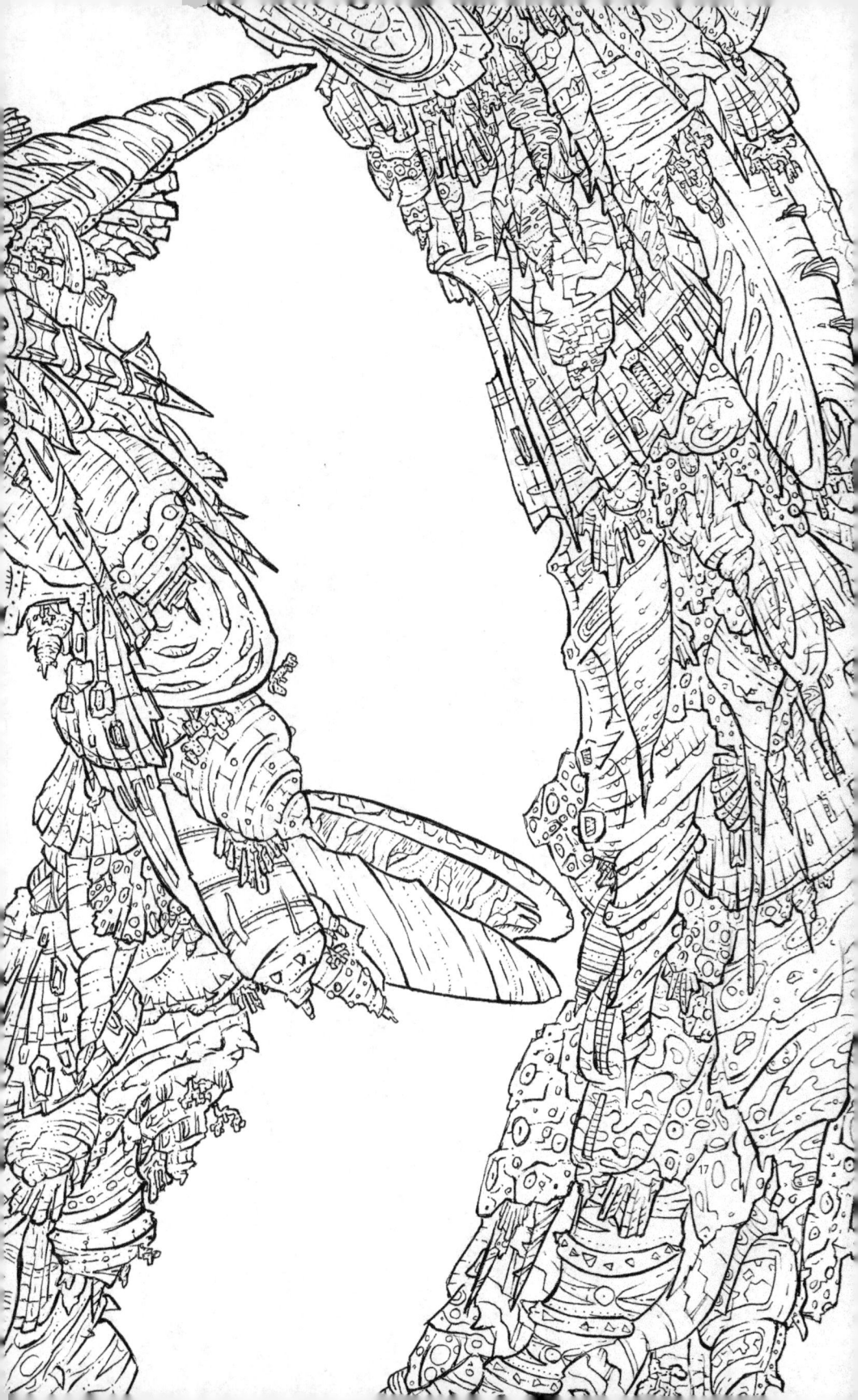

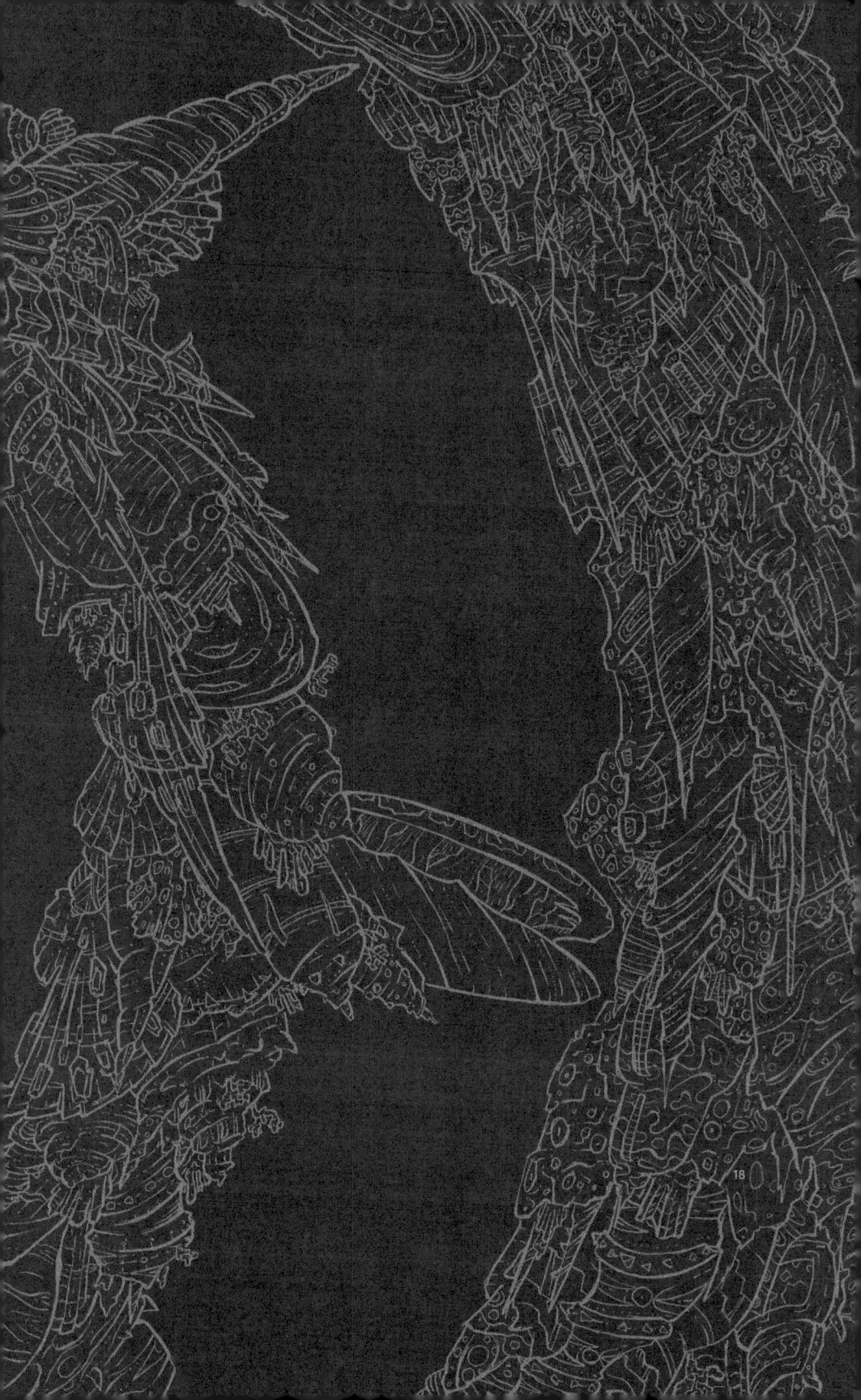

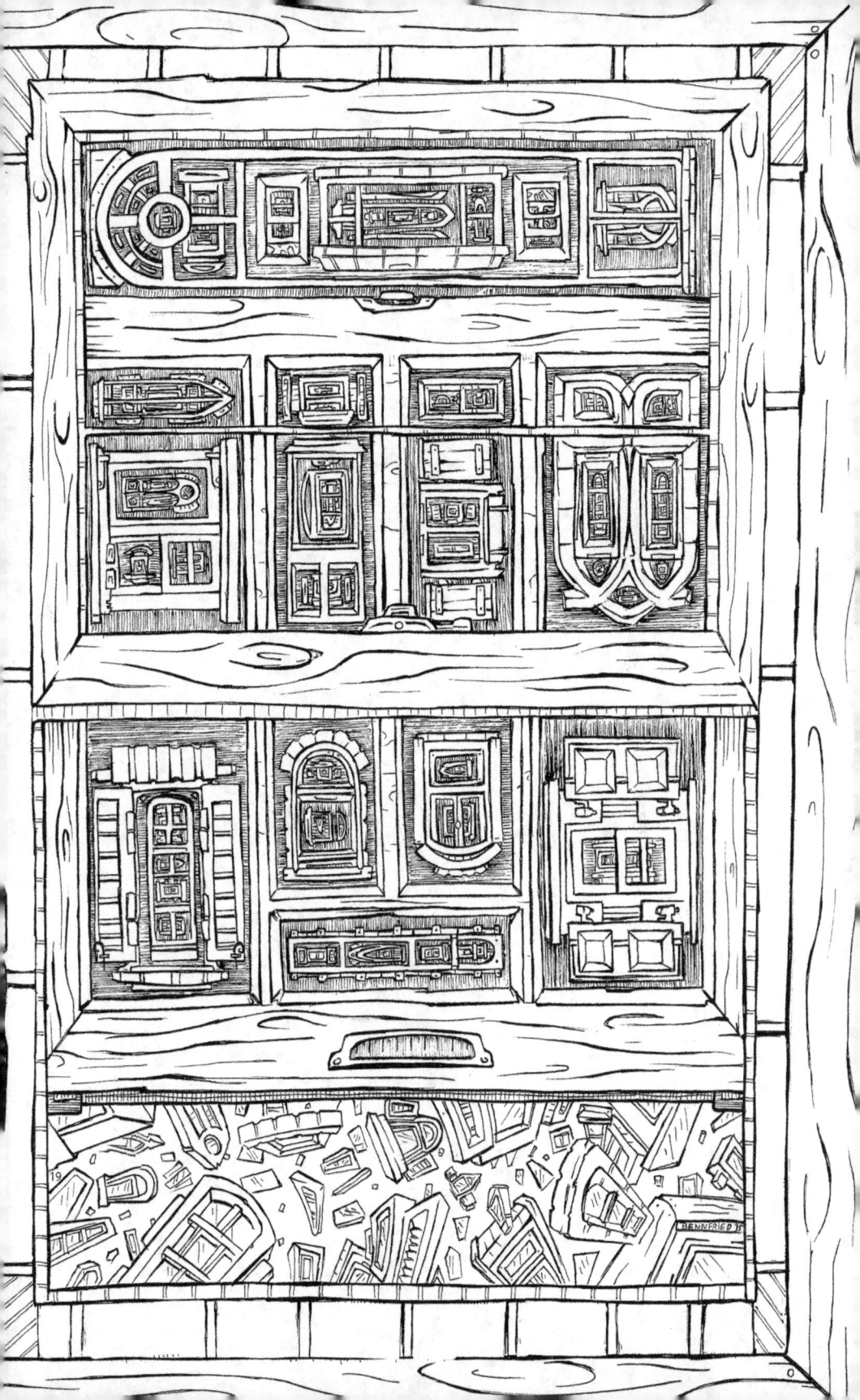

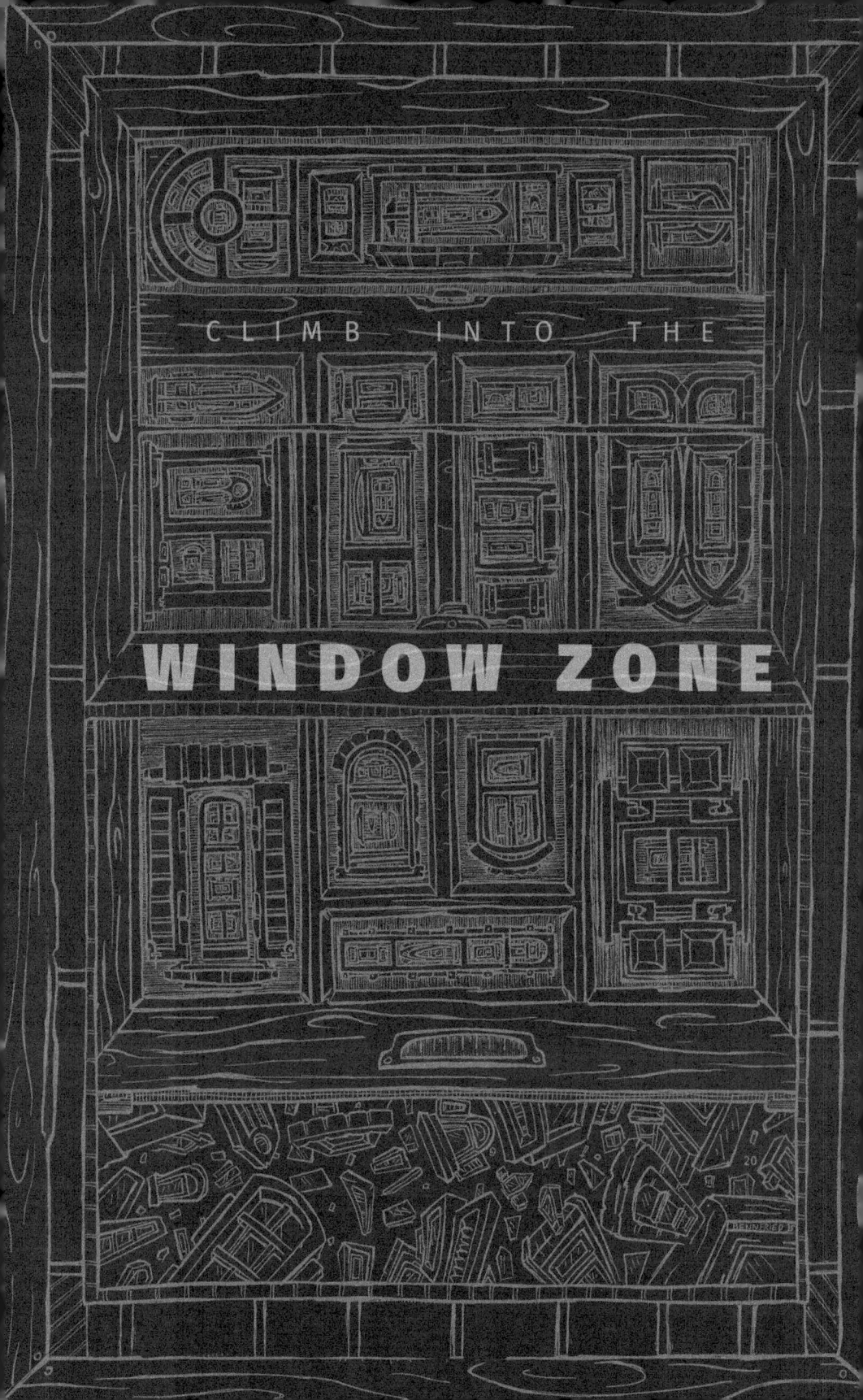

CLIMB INTO THE

WINDOW ZONE

21

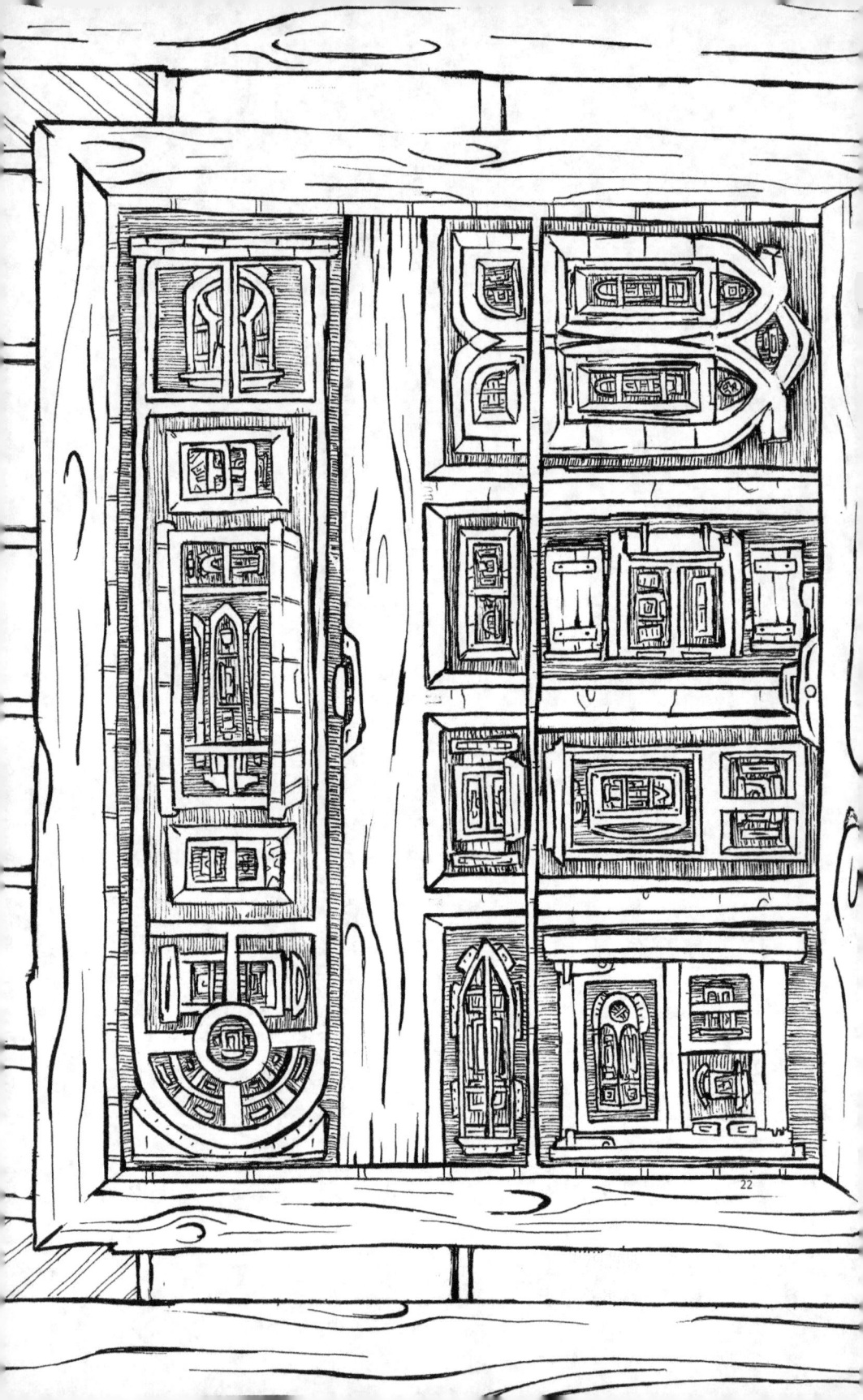

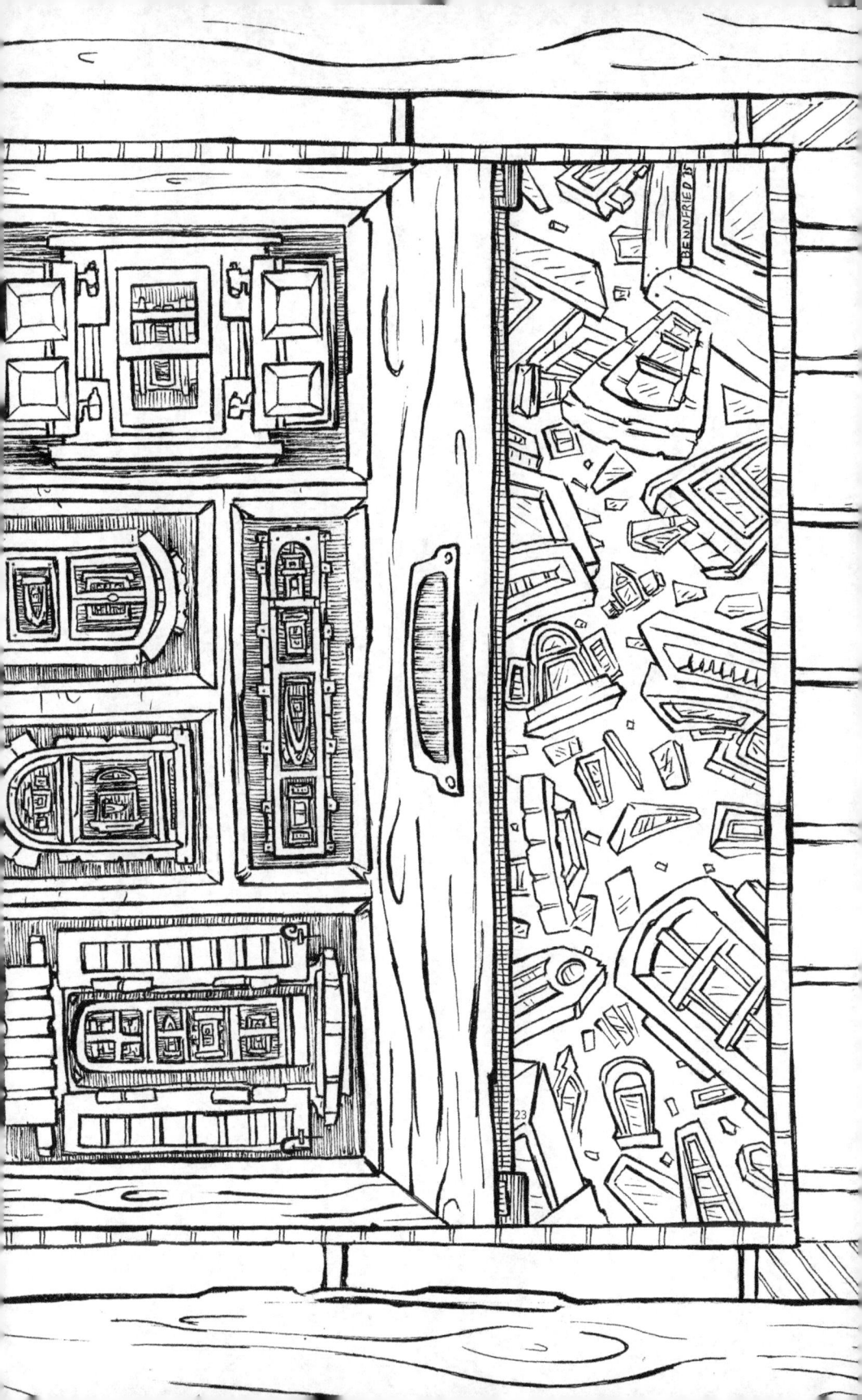

Visit **FriedLines.com** to order a physical copy of this volume, free digital volumes, wallpapers, and more.